JOB EVALUATION IN MUNICIPALITIES

ISBN 87755-164-2

Library of Congress Catalog Card Number 74-189817

1971 $2.50

Studies in Personnel and Management No. 23

JOB EVALUATION IN MUNICIPALITIES

Elizabeth Lanham
Associate Professor of Management

Bureau of Business Research
The University of Texas at Austin

FOREWORD

The Bureau of Business Research is pleased to add, as Number 23 in its series of Studies in Personnel and Management, *JOB EVALUATION IN MUNICIPALITIES* by Elizabeth Lanham, associate professor of management, Graduate School of Business, The University of Texas at Austin.

Dr. Lanham has reexamined, as the first in a series, the findings which she and Dr. William R. Spriegel, then professor of management and dean of the College of Business Administration of The University of Texas, presented in 1955 as Number 9 in the Bureau's Studies in Personnel and Management. Dr. Lanham and Dr. Spriegel collaborated on a series of ten personnel studies during the period from 1951 through 1956, and it is anticipated that the trends in job evaluation in each of the fields surveyed will be reexamined to determine developments during the ensuing years.

Bureau staff members assisting with copy preparation for the publication included Mrs. Linda Brenner, Miss Florence Escott, Mrs. Mary Ann Gready, Charles W. Montfort, Mrs. Glenda Riley, and Daniel P. Rosas. Offset printing was handled by Robert L. Dorsett, assisted by Robert T. Jenkins and Salvador B. Macias.

Stanley A. Arbingast
Director

December 1971

CONTENTS

Chapter   Page

I. Introduction   3
    Scope of the Study   4
    Methodology   4

II. History of Job Evaluation in Municipalities   6
    Status of Job Evaluation   6
    Age of Plans   6
    Reasons for Installing Plans   9

III. Securing the Cooperation of Supervisors
        and Employees   11
    Who Initiated the Programs   11
    Authorization for Conducting Job
        Evaluation Studies   13
    Acquainting the Supervisory Staff
        with the Program   15
    Acquainting Employees with the Program   16
    Type of Information Given to
        Supervisors and Employees   19

IV. Responsibility for Installing the
        Job Evaluation Programs   20
    Source of Personnel for Installations   20
    Reasons for Choice   22
    Supervision of the Installations   24
    Overall Direction of the Installation   25
    Responsibility for Establishing Installations, Main-
        tenance, and Administrative Procedures   28

V. Basic Procedures Performed in Installing the
        Job Evaluation Programs   29
    Rating Methods Used in Municipalities   31
    Reasons for Selecting the Specific Rating Plan   31
    Person or Group Responsible for Selecting
        the Rating Plan   32
    Range of Jobs Rated   33
    Methods Used to Secure Data for
        Job Descriptions   36
    Methods Used and Assignment of Responsibility
        for Training Job Analysts   38
    Assignment of Responsibility for Writing
        Job Descriptions   41
    Assignment of Responsibility for Designing
        the Rating Scale   41
    Assignment of Responsibility for Rating Jobs   45
    Methods Used and Assignment of Responsibility
        for Training Job Raters   47
    Equalization of Job Ratings   49
    Length of Time Required for Installation   50

VI. Measures Taken to Insure Acceptance and Advantages
        Gained from the Program   53
    Securing Approval of Top Management   53
    Securing Acceptance of the Supervisory Group . . .   55
    Presentation of Proposed Plan to Employees   55
    General Experience with the Job
        Evaluation Program   56
    Advantages Secured from the Installation of the
        Job Evaluation Program   58

VII. Maintaining and Controlling the Job
        Evaluation Program   59
    Need for Maintenance and Control   59
    Methods Used to Maintain and
        Control Programs   61

Assignment of Responsibility for
Maintenance and Control 61
Types of Maintenance and Control Exercised 63
Internal Operating Problems Encountered 63
Utilization of Electronic Data Processing for Wage
and Salary Records and Reports 66

VIII. Summary and Conclusions 70
Summary 70
Conclusions.............................. 78

Appendix—Questionnaire 79

LIST OF TABLES

Table   Page

2.1   Reasons for Installing Job Evaluation
       Programs   8
3.1   Source of Original Suggestion for Installation   12
3.2   Methods of Informing Supervisors about Pro-
       posed Studies   15
3.3   Methods of Informing Employees about Pro-
       posed Studies   17
4.1   Reasons for Choice of Assignment for
       Installation   23
4.2   Administrative Area and/or Person Responsible for
       Supervising Job Evaluation Installation   25
4.3   Responsibility for Overall Direction of the
       Program   26
5.1   Reasons for Selecting the Specific Rating
       Plan   32
5.2   Person or Group Responsible for Selecting
       Rating Plan   33
5.3   Methods Used to Secure Information for Job
       Descriptions   37
5.4   Type of Training Given Job Analysts   40
5.5   Responsibility for Writing Final Job
       Descriptions   43
5.6   Responsibility for Rating Jobs   46
5.7   Type of Training Given Job Raters   47
5.8   Responsibility for Equalizing Jobs   50
6.1   Methods Used to Secure Acceptance of the
       Job Evaluation Program   54
6.2   Advantages Secured from Installation of Job
       Evaluation   58

Table   Page

7.1 Methods Used to Maintain and Control Job
        Evaluation Program 60
7.2 Types of Maintenance and Control Exercised by
        Central Control Agency 64
7.3 Internal Operating Problems Encountered in Job
        Evaluation Programs........................ 65
7.4 Wage and Salary Records and Reports Pro-
        cessed Electronically 68

LIST OF FIGURES

Figure   Page

2.1 Status of Job Evaluation   7
2.2 Dates of Installation of Job Evaluation Plans   10
3.1 Source of Authorization of Program   14
3.2 Types of Information Given to Supervisors and Employ-
     ees about the Proposed Job Evaluation Studies   18
4.1 Source of Personnel for Installation   21
4.2 Responsibility for Establishing Installation,
     Maintenance, and Administrative Procedures   27
5.1 Rating Methods Used to Evaluate Jobs   30
5.2 Range of Jobs Evaluated   35
5.3 Responsibility for Securing Information for Job
     Descriptions   39
5.4 Responsibility for Training Job Description
     Interviewers   42
5.5 Responsibility for Designing Scale Used for Rating
     Jobs   44
5.6 Responsibility for Training Raters   48
5.7 Length of Time Required to Establish a Job Evaluation
     Program   51
6.1 Relative Satisfaction with Job Evaluation Programs   57
7.1 Responsibility for Maintenance and Control of Job
     Evaluation Program   62
7.2 Status of EDP Wage and Salary Administration
     Records and Reports   67

JOB EVALUATION IN
MUNICIPALITIES

I

INTRODUCTION

Between 1950 and 1954, eight surveys of job evaluation practices and procedures in various nonindustrial and industrial organizations throughout the United States were sponsored by the Bureau of Business Research, The University of Texas at Austin. Insurance companies, department stores, banks, automotive and automotive-parts industries, aircraft industries, colleges and universities, municipalities, and utility companies were the fields included. Results of each study were published by the Bureau of Business Research in monograph form.

The number of job evaluation programs had grown rapidly in the decade of the 1940's. However, relatively little published material covering detailed studies of job evaluation practices in specific fields of operation were available in the early 1950's. The primary purpose of the above monographs, therefore, was to help fill the existing gap. The monographs, taken as a whole, provided a fairly broad study of many American organizations. Individually, the monographs covered existing practices in the respective fields.

In the spring of 1970, the decision was made to reexamine trends in job evaluation practices in order to determine what had occurred in the intervening years. Municipalities were selected as the first group to study. The rapid growth of many cities, with their mushrooming number of employees and attendant problems of wage and salary administration for these employees, suggested this group as a worthwhile one to examine first.

Scope of the Study

The six major topics discussed in this monograph are (a) history of job evaluation in municipalities, (b) methods used in securing the cooperation of supervisors and employees, (c) assignment of responsibility for the job evaluation installation, (d) organization for and conduct of the installation, (e) measures taken to insure acceptance and advantages gained from the programs, and (f) procedures followed in maintaining and controlling the plans and utilization of electronic processing of wage and salary records and reports.

The six areas reexamine the same basic topics surveyed in the original study with one exception. In the last area, procedures followed in maintaining and controlling the plans, the section on utilization of electronic data-processing of wage and salary reports and records has been added. A significant trend in this direction has occurred in many nonindustrial and industrial organizations throughout the country in the last decade. The inclusion of the subject reveals the status of such EDP development in municipalities.

Methodology

To secure information about these six areas, a six-page questionnaire (see Appendix A) accompanied by a letter of explanation was sent to the personnel directors of 76 widely scattered municipalities, each of which had a population of at least 125,000. Sixty-eight (87 percent) replied to the inquiry. Of this number, 51 (75 percent) had formal plans of job evaluation in effect. The procedures and practices followed by these 51 cities serve as the basis for this study. In addition, comparisons between

1954 and 1970 practices are included in order to point out similarities and differences between the two time periods.

II

HISTORY OF JOB EVALUATION
IN MUNICIPALITIES

Status of Job Evaluation

Fifty-one of the 68 respondents (75 percent) reported formal plans of job evaluation. One more was currently installing a formal plan at the time of the survey while another was definitely planning to install one in the near future. Thus, 53 of the cities have, or soon might have, such programs. Only seven stated that they had neither a job evaluation program nor any plan to install one. Eight cities used informal methods for determining job worth. (See Figure 2.1.)

In 1954, a response was received from 57 cities (75 percent) of the total receiving the questionnaire. Twenty-eight (49 percent) of those were found to have formal plans. Thus, the adoption of such programs in municipalities of 125,000 population and over has increased approximately 26 percent since that time.

Age of Plans

Formal job evaluation programs were established in about the same number of municipalities in both the 1950's and 1960's. (See Figure 2.2.) Fifteen plans were adopted in the former decade and 16 in the latter. The decade of the forties was the third period of greatest activity in that 10 were reported for that span of time. The fourth major period of growth occurred between 1930 and 1939 with 7 falling within that range. Two of the cities had plans prior to 1930, and one completed its program as recently as 1970. Thus, the development of job evaluation programs in municipal government began at an early date and is still continuing.

Figure 2.1

STATUS OF JOB EVALUATION

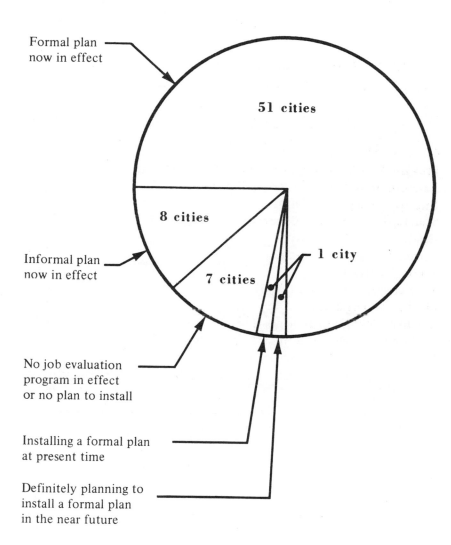

Formal plan now in effect

51 cities

8 cities

Informal plan now in effect

7 cities

1 city

No job evaluation program in effect or no plan to install

Installing a formal plan at present time

Definitely planning to install a formal plan in the near future

Table 2.1

REASONS FOR INSTALLING JOB EVALUATION PROGRAMS

Reason	Number of cities
Create equity in salary administration	49
Provide definite, systematic, and factual data for determining the relative worth of jobs	48
Improve salary administration	42
Standardize salary administration	41
Establish a basis for promotion	38
Increase employee morale	27
Control salary cost	25
Reduce grievances and turnover	21
Meet legal requirement	4
Establish relationship of positions	1
Update and upgrade examination content and validity	1
Meet needs of civil service system	1
Total	298*

* Some cities indicated more than one reason.

Reasons for Installing Plans

Eight major reasons were given for installing the job evaluation plans. (See Table 2.1.) In most cases, several purposes were reported to be factors underlying the installation. All but two of these eight objectives were named by at least one-half of the respondents. The other two were reported by a little less than one-half.

The same major reasons for installation were reported in 1954. However, their rank order in terms of number of times checked altered slightly between 1954 and 1970. To create equity in salary administration, to provide definite, systematic, and factual data, to improve salary administration, and to standardize salary administration were the top four reasons cited in 1970. In the 1954 study, to create equity in salary administration, to provide definite, systematic, and factual data, and to establish a basis for promotion tied for first place with 22 cities reporting each of the reasons. To establish a basis of promotion, one of the top three reasons in 1954, dropped to fifth rank in 1970. It is still an important reason since 38 of the 51 cities cited it, but it is now superseded by the desire to improve and to standardize salary administration. Controlling salary costs and reducing grievances and turnover still are reported as underlying factors in fewer cases than were any of the other purposes cited. To increase employee morale was given a higher rank order in 1954 than was improving salary administration. In 1970, increasing employee morale dropped to sixth place with only controlling salary costs and reducing grievances and turnover falling below its level.

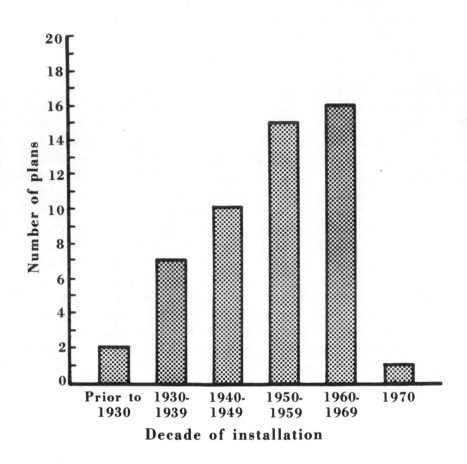

Figure 2.2

DATES OF INSTALLATION OF
JOB EVALUATION PLANS

III

SECURING THE COOPERATION OF SUPERVISORS AND EMPLOYEES

Who Initiated the Programs

In the field of municipal government, management has been primarily responsible for initiating the idea of establishing a program of job evaluation. Nonsupervisory employees originated the suggestion for installation in one city. The above trend of management initiative also was found in 1954. Although employees generally have become more vocal in expressing their desires in the intervening years, they apparently have not yet taken the direct initiative in this area of operation. It is possible, however, that employee concern about inequities in pay, as expressed in their complaints and grievances, may have led members of management to suggest methods for correction. Thus, their influence upon establishing programs may have been of an indirect rather than a direct nature. Of course, progressive and knowledgeable managers move forward in supporting programs which offer a better solution to problems without waiting for the initiative of employees. The fact that 75 percent of a rather large sample of cities from a broad geographical area had formal

11

programs indicated that their management personnel recognized the need for and had implemented these highly desirable plans.

No one person or group served as the primary originator of the idea. The personnel manager, either alone or with others, however, was named more frequently than anyone else. The pattern was generally varied and included such persons as the city manager, the mayor, the city council, and the civil service board or commission. Some respondents stated that the city charter or other legislative action led to the establishment. (See Table 3.1.)

Table 3.1

SOURCE OF ORIGINAL SUGGESTION FOR INSTALLATION

Source	Number of cities
Personnel manager	14
City charter	6
City manager	5
Civil service board or commission	3
Legislation	3
Outside consultant	2
Mayor	1
Personnel manager and salary commission	1
Nonsupervisory employees	1
Management survey	1
City council	1
Personnel policy board	1
Civil service director	1
Director	1
Unknown	10
Total	51

The fact that personnel managers most frequently suggest job evaluation studies appears to be a natural and logical development.

Job evaluation is usually one of the functions or activities of a personnel department. Also, a progressive personnel manager generally is familiar with job evaluation techniques and advantages of such programs. Finally, a personnel manager normally should be one of the first to realize such a need because of his constant contact with employee grievances and complaints regarding wages.

Authorization for Conducting Job Evaluation Studies

Any program with such a far-reaching effect on operations as that of job evaluation ordinarily must have the approval and support of top management in order to operate successfully. When an organization adopts a formal method of classifying its jobs and then prices those jobs with respect to their relative positions in the classification, that organization is committing itself to a definite plan of procedure and operation. This does not mean that such a program is rigidly inflexible. It does mean, however, that any proposed changes which bring about a deviation from the plan must be scrutinized with care and attention and prove to be defensible before the changes are allowed. Otherwise, the program becomes invalid.

Examined, then, from the standpoint of both present and future operation, an organization commits itself to proceed according to an established program when job evaluation is adopted. Such a decision is one that should rest with the top policy-making group.

Although different persons or groups at the top level of management were responsible for authorizing the studies, the upper echelons fulfilled their obligation as recommended above. (See Figure 3.1.) The city council or comparable body granted the authority in more cases than any other source. A city charter or other legislation provided the authority in 14 cities. The civil service commission alone or with the city council was the next most commonly cited group. The remaining sources, although varied in title, still supported the trend of management's responsibility for authorization.

13

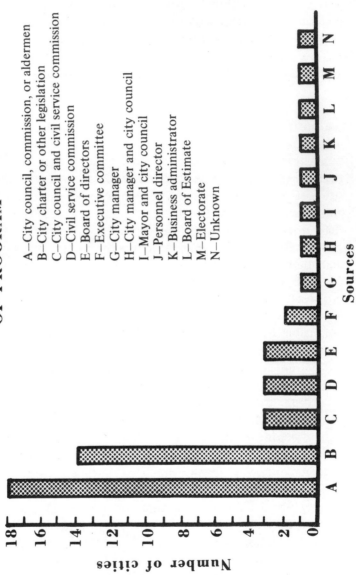

Figure 3.1

SOURCE OF AUTHORIZATION OF PROGRAM

A–City council, commission, or aldermen
B–City charter or other legislation
C–City council and civil service commission
D–Civil service commission
E–Board of directors
F–Executive committee
G–City manager
H–City manager and city council
I–Mayor and city council
J–Personnel director
K–Business administrator
L–Board of Estimate
M–Electorate
N–Unknown

Table 3.2

METHODS OF INFORMING SUPERVISORS
ABOUT PROPOSED STUDIES

Method	Number of cities
Staff meetings	35
Conferences with individual staff members	31
Departmental group meetings	25
Letter or memorandum from city head	18
Letter or memorandum from personnel department	2
Civil service rules	1
Staff reports	1
Special bulletins	1
No answer	6
Total	120*

* Some municipalities indicated more than one method.

The situation has not changed since 1954. The cities which have established their programs since that time have followed their predecessors in this respect.

Acquainting the Supervisory Staff with the Program

The adoption of systematic uniform control of salary administration is a step that requires considerable care. A formal plan of administration requires that each supervisor administering it conform to certain policies and be subject to certain checks. There is usually greater freedom for the supervisor under the informal approach. The formal one means that supervisors will no longer be in a position to act with their usual freedom. Therefore, their cooperation and support must be gained if the newly developed program is to be successful.

Four primary methods were used in the attempt to secure the cooperation of the supervisory group. (See Table 3.2.) Many of the respondents indicated that more than one method was utilized. Both staff meetings and individual conferences were used by over one-half of the respondents. Slightly less than one-half conducted departmental group meetings, while the heads of one-third of the cities sent out letters or memos about the program in order to help inform its supervisory staff. These same four methods also were the primary ones followed in 1954.

It is evident from the above that both then and now the need for securing the cooperation and support of the supervisory group was recognized. Often more than one method had been utilized. In addition, the personal approach had been followed widely rather than relying primarily upon written communications.

Acquainting Employees with the Program

Not only is the cooperation and support of the supervisory staff needed but that of employees is also highly desirable if a job evaluation plan is to serve its full purpose and result in a satisfactory salary structure. Employees must understand why such a program has been set up and how it will affect them.

Of the eight procedures named by more than one respondent for accomplishing this purpose, six were followed by at least one-third of the group. These six in order of popularity were (a) information from supervisors or department heads, (b) individual conferences, (c) group meetings, (d) letter or memorandum from city head, (e) conferences with employee leaders, and (f) special bulletins. (See Table 3.3.)

An analysis of the practices for acquainting both supervisors and employees reveals that the personal approach was more popular than the impersonal one. Meetings, on an individual or group basis or both, outnumbered the instances where printed matter alone was. used. Where printed matter was used, it

16

Table 3.3

METHODS OF INFORMING EMPLOYEES
ABOUT PROPOSED STUDIES

Method	Number of cities
Information from supervisors or department heads	32
Individual conferences	27
Group meetings	24
Letter or memorandum from city head	23
Conferences with employee leaders	17
Special bulletins and staff reports	17
Union representatives	14
Employee publications	9
Job audits	1
Job descriptions	1
Letter or memorandum from personnel department	1
Employee council	1
No answer	5
Total	172*

* Some municipalities indicated more than one method.

supplemented other procedures of the personal contact type. Apparently, the belief is that such an important undertaking as that of informing supervisors and employees justified the time, effort, and expense of the personal approach.

The same situation was found in the 1954 study. Cities at that time also relied primarily on the same type of personal approaches to inform both groups.

Figure 3.2

TYPES OF INFORMATION GIVEN TO SUPERVISORS AND EMPLOYEES ABOUT THE PROPOSED JOB EVALUATION STUDIES

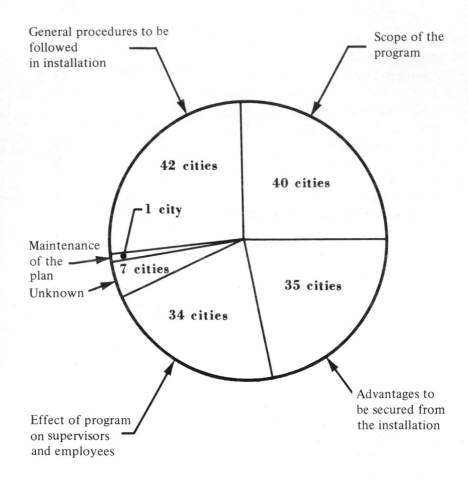

(Some municipalities indicated that more than one type of information was communicated.)

Type of Information Given to Supervisors and Employees

Four major areas were covered by the respondents in disseminating information about their job evaluation programs. Well over half reviewed the general procedures to be followed in installing the plan as well as its scope, advantages, and effect upon both supervisors and employees. (See Figure 3.2.)

It is evident that the majority of these organizations not only used the personal approach in presenting information but, in addition, provided a relatively broad coverage in the type of information given. Both of the above procedures are highly recommended by authorities in the field for securing understanding and cooperation from both groups. The same practices prevailed in 1954.

IV

RESPONSIBILITY FOR INSTALLING
THE JOB EVALUATION PROGRAMS

After an organization has decided to install a job evaluation program, administrative arrangements for carrying out the installation must be made. The assignments of responsibility made by these municipalities are reviewed below in order to reveal their organizational practices.

Source of Personnel for Installations

One of the first problems is to determine whether to assign the installation to employees of the organization, to assign it to a management consulting firm, or to combine the two sources in some way. In the case of combining employees and consultants, two major approaches are possible. The first is to assign the primary responsibility to the employees but hire a management consulting firm to aid them in their work. The second is to assign the primary responsibility to the consulting firm but use employees to aid it.

20

Figure 4.1

SOURCE OF PERSONNEL
FOR INSTALLATION

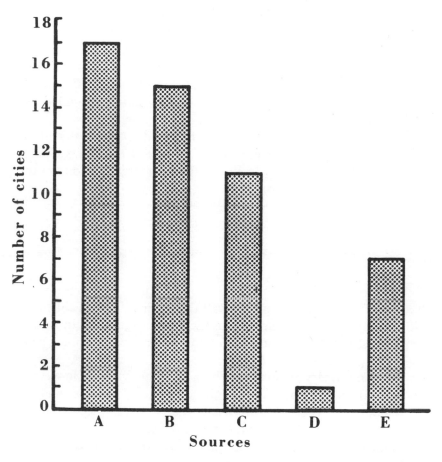

A—Management consultant firm aided by employees
B—Employees without aid of management consultant firm
C—Employees with aid of management consultant firm
D—Management consulting firm exclusively
E—No answer

In making the selection, an organization should examine carefully each of the approaches and should weigh its advantages and disadvantages against the problems of installation which confront it. Such an examination may reveal the one method which best fits its needs.

Employees of the cities played the dominant role in installation. Either they were charged with the entire responsibility (15 cities), or they were in charge but had the assistance of consultants (11 cities). Thus, they carried the primary responsibility in 26, or slightly over one-half, of the municipalities. By comparison, consultants alone or aided by employees were in charge in 18 cities. (See Figure 4.1.)

The above trend differs from that found in 1954. At that time, management consultants were in the dominant role. This change now brings the cities more in line with other organizations in the assignment of such responsibility.

Reasons for Choice

Most of the respondents gave more than one reason for choosing a particular group to install the program. (See Table 4.1.) The exception was the one city using the management consultant firm exclusively. In that case the reason or reasons for choice were not indicated.

The two primary reasons for choosing employees alone were as follows: (a) the employees knew the organization better than did an outsider, and (b) the employees were well qualified to install the plan. In the case of combining employees and consultants, the two primary reasons were: (a) such a method provided both for the knowledge of the organization as held by employees and for the technical skill of the consultants, and (b) such a method permitted employee participation but maintained the objective viewpoint of the consultant.

The same two major reasons for utilizing employees to install the program as well as combining employees and consultants were

22

Table 4.1

REASONS FOR CHOICE OF ASSIGNMENT FOR INSTALLATION

Employees	Number of cities
Knew organization better than outsider	13
Well qualified to install program	12
Participation aided in acceptance and understanding	6
Trained group for maintenance of program	4
Reduced suspicion toward plan	2
Total	37*

Employees and consultant	
Knowledge of organization combined with technical skill	24
Allowed employee participation, and maintained objective point of view	18
Required less time than employees working alone	9
Provided dual evaluation of final results	1
Reduced costs	1
Greater employee acceptance than with consultants working alone	1
Trained employees for maintenance when consultants no longer available	1
Total	55*

* Some municipalities indicated more than one reason on their choice of assignment.

reported by the respondents in 1954. However, since employees were found to be in the more dominant role in 1970, it is possible that employees are now more knowledgeable about job evaluation and do not need the degree of help from the consulting firms which they did at an earlier date.

Another slight change between the 1954 and 1970 practices occured in the rank order of the two primary reasons given for combining employees and consultants to install the plan. In 1954, "allowing employee participation plus maintaining an objective point of view" was reported by more cities than those which cited "knowledge of organization combined with technical skill." In 1970, the combination of "organizational and technical knowledge" led with more respondents checking it then checked "participation plus objectivity."

In the case of utilizing employees alone, the same number of cities reported the two reasons in 1954. In 1970, one more city reported "selecting employees because they knew the organization better than outsiders" than selected the second reason of "well qualified to install program."

Supervision of the Installations

In a large majority of the municipalities (43 out of 51), overall responsibility for supervising the job evaluation installation was assigned to the personnel department. (See Table 4.2.) In three other cities this assignment was given to a combination of either the personnel department and city manager, the personnel department and common council, or the personnel department and the organization department. These three combination assignments, plus the 43 personnel departments supervising the programs alone, indicate that in all but five cities the personnel area performed a very active role in administering the installations.

Personnel departments also were found to be the major area of assignment of supervisory responsibility in the 1954 survey. Seventeen of the 28 respondents reported that personnel

Table 4.2

**ADMINISTRATIVE AREA AND/OR PERSON RESPONSIBLE
FOR SUPERVISING JOB EVALUATION INSTALLATION**

Area	Number of cities
Personnel department	43
Personnel department and city manager	1
Personnel department and common council	1
Personnel department and organization department	1
City manager	1
Civil service department	1
No answer	3
Total	51

departments alone had the responsibility. Two others indicated the personnel department combined either with a budget committee or with the office manager exercised this function. However, 8 of the 28 cities in that survey had areas other than personnel supervise the installation. Thus, the trend toward personnel department assignment has grown stronger since 1954.

Assigning supervisory responsibility for installing the program to the personnel department is in accord with the procedures generally recommended by job evaluation experts. The general opinion is that the personnel department should play the dominant role. This assignment is logical because job evaluation is closely related to some other areas of work usually performed by the personnel department, e.g., wage and salary administration.

Overall Direction of the Installation

The direction of the installation was most commonly assigned to the personnel director (19 cities). (See Table 4.3.) Consultants

Table 4.3

RESPONSIBILITY FOR OVERALL DIRECTION OF THE PROGRAM

Title	Number of cities
Personnel director	19
Consultant	12
Civil service department	5
City manager	2
Citizens advisory group	1
Analyst	1
No answer	11
Total	51

directed the installations in nine cities while the civil service board performed this role in five cities and the city manager in two. One respondent indicated that a citizens advisory board directed its program, and another placed an analyst in charge. Since the personnel department had overall responsibility for supervising the installation, it is logical that the director of personnel also would direct the program in many cities, although this was not always the case as indicated above.

Personnel directors were not responsible for overall direction to nearly the same degree in 1954 as they were in 1970. Consultants, civil service boards, and public administration service groups were among those primarily responsible in the earlier installations. Here, as in the previously discussed areas, the personnel director and his department or staff are far more active in supervising and directing job evaluation programs than they were some sixteen years ago.

Figure 4.2

RESPONSIBILITY FOR ESTABLISHING INSTALLATION, MAINTENANCE, AND ADMINISTRATIVE PROCEDURES

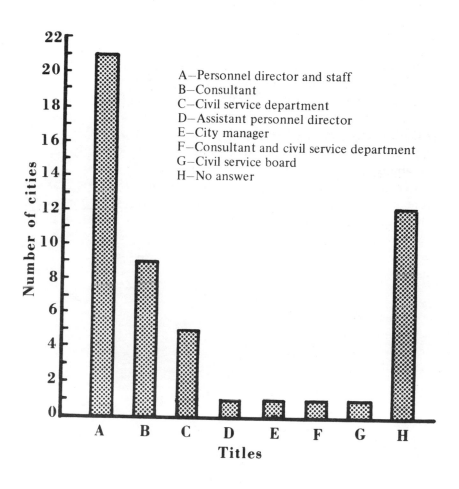

A—Personnel director and staff
B—Consultant
C—Civil service department
D—Assistant personnel director
E—City manager
F—Consultant and civil service department
G—Civil service board
H—No answer

Responsibility for Establishing Installations, Maintenance, and Administrative Procedures

Those responsible for overall direction of the installation usually were assigned responsibility for establishing installations, maintenance, and administrative procedures. (See Figure 4.2.) However, a slight variation occurred. The personnel director and his staff handled these areas in 21 cities as compared with 19 personnel directors who also exercised overall direction. Twelve consultants were in overall charge of the program, but nine were listed as responsible for establishing the above procedures. Two city managers exercised overall direction, but one of these delegated procedure responsibility to someone else. The assistant personnel director, civil service department and consultant, and a civil service board served their cities in this capacity in the remaining cases.

Those in charge of overall direction of the 1954 programs also were responsible in most cities for procedures at that time. Although this was not always the case, the small variation in the trend is not significant.

V

BASIC PROCEDURES PERFORMED IN INSTALLING THE JOB EVALUATION PROGRAMS

In installing a program of job evaluation, certain basic procedures must be performed. In addition, these procedures generally need to be carried out in sequential order since one stage of development often depends upon either prior or concurrent execution of other steps. For example, a rating plan must be selected, job facts secured, job descriptions written, jobs rated and classifed, pay rates determined, and administrative policies established. Job descriptions cannot be written until job facts are secured. Jobs cannot be rated and classified until a rating plan is selected. The rate structure cannot be determined before jobs are rated and classified and so on for the respective procedures. Of course, the rating plan may be in the process of being developed while job facts are being secured and job descriptions written. It must be ready for use, however, when job descriptions are completed if unnecessary delays are to be avoided.

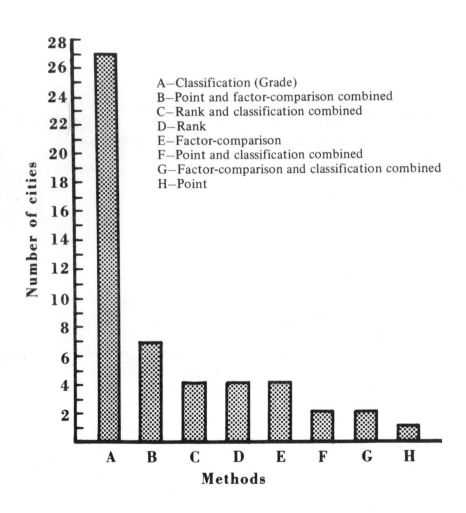

Figure 5.1
RATING METHODS USED
TO EVALUATE JOBS

A—Classification (Grade)
B—Point and factor-comparison combined
C—Rank and classification combined
D—Rank
E—Factor-comparison
F—Point and classification combined
G—Factor-comparison and classification combined
H—Point

Certain phases of the respondents' programs are reviewed below in order to show the specific procedures used in executing the major steps.

Rating Methods Used in Municipalities

Over half of the municipalities (27) used the classification (grade) method for evaluating their jobs. Eight more combined it with elements of the rank, point, or factor-comparison methods. Thus, 35 cities employed the procedure to some degree. None of the other three methods came even close to it in popularity. (See Figure 5.1.)

In frequency of use nationally, the classification method ranks third. The reversal of trend found here possibly results from the fact that civil service jobs in the federal government are evaluated by the classification method.

The classification method was used also in over half the cities in rating jobs in plans studied in 1954. It was either used alone or was combined with one of the other three plans as found in the 1970 survey. Its popularity then and now probably is due to the reason given above.

Reasons for Selecting the Specific Rating Plan

The leading reason for the selection of a specific rating plan was suitability to the needs of the city. (See Table 5.1.) Three other reasons tied for second place; (1) the plan was used by other cities: (2) the plan could be understood more easily by employees; and (3) the plan was recommended by a consultant. Fewer problems of administration and more information about the plan were cited by 11 and 8 respondents, respectively. The remaining bases of choice were cited in too few cases to show any particular trend. The same basic reasons predominated the choice in 1954.

31

Table 5.1

REASONS FOR SELECTING THE SPECIFIC RATING PLAN

Reason	Number of cities
Better suited to city needs	36
Used by other cities	19
More easily understood by employees	19
Recommended by consultant	19
Fewer problems of administration	11
More information about plan	8
More accurate and equitable than others although more complete	1
Easier to justify	1
Recommended by managerial and technical committee	1
Recommended by personnel director and civil service commission	1
Required by law	1
Lower cost	1
General popularity and acceptance in private industry	1
Practical and better acceptance by municipal hospital employees	1
Total	120*

* Some municipalities indicated more than one reason.

Person or Group Responsible for Selecting the Rating Plan

The personnel director or a consultant, either assisted by others or operating alone, made the actual selection of the job rating plan in more cities than did any other person or group. In 14 cities the responsibility was assigned to the personnel director alone or with assistance from others. (See Table 5.2.) It was assigned to the consultant alone or assisted by others in 13 cities. A combination of the personnel director and a consultant served one city. The remaining assignments were made in too few cases to be of significance.

The consultant alone or aided by others selected the rating plan in more cities than did anyone else in the plans reviewed in 1954. The rise in the number of personnel directors participating in this role in 1970 parallels their present greater involvement in overall direction, supervision, and maintenance of job evaluations plans.

Table 5.2

PERSON OR GROUP RESPONSIBLE FOR SELECTING RATING PLAN

Person or group	Number of cities
Personnel director alone or assisted by others	14
Consultant alone or assisted by others	13
Civil service department	3
Personnel director and consultant	1
Joint group	1
Classification analyst	1
No answer	18
Total	51

Range of Jobs Rated

Early in the planning stage of a job evaluation program it is necessary to determine what jobs are to be included because the design of the rating plan is affected by the levels of jobs to be rated. For example, more gradations of level normally would be needed in a classification system used to rate jobs from the beginning through the top executive level than would be necessary to cover jobs from the beginning level through the department head level only. Also, certain factors as well as degrees of the factors often need to be added in the point method if beginning jobs through top-level jobs are to be rated than if the range stops at the department-head level. The rating method, therefore, needs to be designed in such a way that it provides a measure of the levels of work to be evaluated.

In the early days of installation, a majority of organizations included up to or through the department-head level only. One reason often given for excluding higher-level jobs was that they were much harder to evaluate than those in lower levels. Personal ambition, ability, and personality were thought to have influenced the scope of a particular executive's job to such an extent that separating actual job requirements from the incumbent's aptitude seemed an insurmountable task. Another reason expressed rather widely was that since there were so few top-level jobs in an organization as compared with the number in the lower levels, they could be handled on an individual basis and did not impose the problems induced by the sheer magnitude of the many in the lower echelons. A third commonly cited reason for excluding high level jobs was that job evaluation techniques were new and should be "tried out" first on the more routine jobs which seemed easier to evaluate. The reasoning seemed to be that when sound procedures had been developed, an extension could then be made to more complex jobs.

Ratings of beginning jobs through the department or division head jobs (21 cities), followed by ratings of beginning jobs through the top executive level (18 cities), and, finally, ratings of beginning jobs and up to, but not including, department or division heads (12 cities) was the rank order of popularity of the ranges included in these job evaluation programs. (See Figure 5.2.) The rank order is the same as the one found in the 1954 survey. Despite the growth in the number of installations and the many years of experience with plans in many cities, the top echelon is

Figure 5.2
RANGE OF JOBS EVALUATED

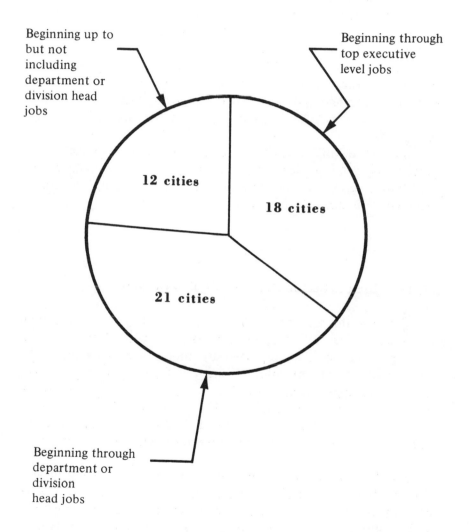

Beginning up to but not including department or division head jobs

Beginning through top executive level jobs

12 cities

18 cities

21 cities

Beginning through department or division head jobs

still excluded in about the same percentage of cities now as in 1954. A slight decline in the percentage of cities rating through the department or division head level has occurred since 1954. In that survey, 46 percent rated through the department head or division head level as compared with 41 percent in 1970. The decline has not occurred because a larger percentage are going higher; instead, it has occurred because a larger percentage are rating up to but not through department and division heads. The percentage change is small but interesting in that it was predicted in the early days of job evaluation that top level jobs would be included more and more as experience with plans was acquired. The prediction has not become reality in the field of municipal government.

In most of the cities, the person or group responsible for procedures, maintenance, and administration of the installations was also responsible for determining the range of jobs to be included. The same was true in 1954.

Methods Used to Secure Data for Job Descriptions

Many of the respondents indicated that they used more than one method for collecting information about job duties. The six most popular ones, all reported by more than one-half of the participants, were (a) interviewing employees on the job, (b) interviewing supervisors of the job, (c) questionnaires filled in by employees, (d) questionnaires filled in by and interviews with employees, (e) questionnaires filled in by supervisors, and (f) questionnaires filled in by and interviews with supervisors. (See Table 5.3.)

Job descriptions written by employees and by supervisors were also relatively popular practices. The remaining methods were cited by one respondent each except for the "questionnaire filled in by employee and reviewed by supervisor and/or department head," which was reported twice.

36

Table 5.3

METHODS USED TO SECURE INFORMATION
FOR JOB DESCRIPTIONS

Method	Number of cities
Interviewing employees on job	36
Interviewing supervisor of job	34
Questionnaire filled in by employee	31
Questionnaire and interview from employee	29
Questionnaire filled in by supervisor	26
Questionnaire and interview from supervisor	26
Job description written by department head	21
Job description written by employee	18
Questionnaire filled in by employee and reviewed by supervisor and/or department head	2
Job description written by employee and reviewed by supervisor	1
Interviewing sample group of employees	1
Questionnaires filled in by job analysts	1
Observation of jobs	1
Data partially from annual reports, budgets, equipment inventories, etc.	1
Civil service department	1
Cross comparisons	1
No answer	8
Total	238*

* Some municipalities reported more than one method.

Interviewing employees and supervisors is highly recommended for securing job facts because more accurate and complete information usually can be secured. Questionnaires followed by interviews are recommended over the use of questionnaires alone. Employee and supervisory participation in the procedure is also considered to be a better approach than either one alone. Job facts in these cities generally have been secured according to recommended practice.

The personnel director or consultant, either working alone or assisted by others, was primarily responsible for securing job facts. (See Figure 5.3.) If the personnel director, personnel department, personnel director and the consultant, director and personnel, and assistant personnel director are grouped together because each includes the term personnel, 17, or one-third of the assignments, were in the personnel area. The consultant either alone or with others was named by 12, or slightly over one-fourth, of the respondents as carrying the primary responsibility. The civil service department served in five cities, the classification analyst in five others. The remaining assignments occurred in one city each.

Members of the personnel department and consultants also performed the function in more of the cities in 1954. However, the personnel director and his staff were more active in 1970 than in 1954.

The title of job analyst (classification analyst) was not used widely in either of the surveys although it is the term commonly used to designate the person securing job facts. The reason may be that the person named also performed other duties. Thus, the title used may be more descriptive of all functions performed than would have been the case had the title of job analyst been adopted.

Methods Used and Assignment of Responsibility
for Training Job Analysts

Five different methods for training those responsible for securing job facts were reported by at least one-third or more of

Figure 5.3

RESPONSIBILITY FOR SECURING INFORMATION FOR JOB DESCRIPTIONS

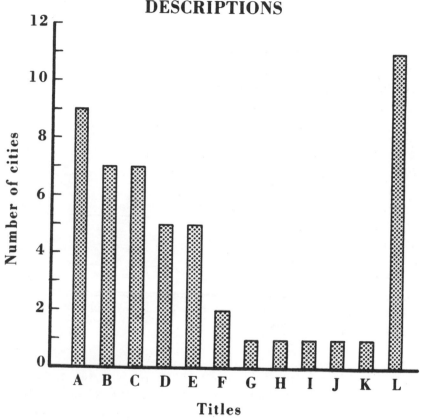

A—Consultant
B—Personnel director
C—Personnel department
D—Civil service department
E—Classification analyst
F—Consultant and staff

G—Personnel director and consultant
H—Assistant personnel director
I—Citizens group and wage and salary committee
J—Department heads
K—Director and personnel
L—No answer

39

Table 5.4

TYPE OF TRAINING GIVEN JOB ANALYSTS

Type	Number of cities
Studied job evaluation literature	32
Learned procedures for getting job facts	32
Learned principles of interviewing	21
Prepared sample job descriptions which were criticized	20
Took university courses	19
Visited other cities with job evaluation plans	1
Conducted orientation, conferences, and on-the-job training	1
Applied principles and techniques in a supervised setting	1
Had prior training and experience	3
Total	130*

* Some cities gave more than one type of training while three utilized previously trained personnel.

the respondents. (See Table 5.4.) These five were (a) studied job evaluation literature, (b) learned procedures for getting job facts, (c) learned principles of interviewing, (d) prepared sample job descriptions which were criticized, and (e) took university courses.

The same five primary methods were found in 1954. The rank order of importance of the methods differs slightly, however, between the two periods. For example, "reliance upon university courses" was in the last rank order in the 1970 survey but in rank three in 1954. The relative change in the ranks is so minor, however, that no new trend is evident.

40

Consultants and personnel directors either alone or with staff assistance were cited most frequently as having the responsibility for training those who were to secure job facts. (See Figure 5.4.) Consultants were named by more respondents than personnel directors in both the 1954 and the 1970 studies. However, the personnel director and his staff were more active in training by 1970 than in the preceding period. This trend has been found also in a number of other activities as mentioned previously.

Assignment of Responsibility for Writing Job Descriptions

When job facts have been secured, the next step is to write the job descriptions. Members of the personnel department and consultants, named with almost equal frequency, were the two primary groups which performed this step. (See Table 5.5.) The same person or group who secured job facts also wrote the final job descriptions in many of the cities. Having the same persons perform both tasks is common practice because those who secure the information usually are better informed about the job. The above trend was found also in 1954.

Although it is generally a recommended practice to have final job descriptions approved by both the supervisor of the job and the employee on the job in order to improve accuracy and acceptance, job descriptions were submitted to supervisors only in most of the cities. Now, as in 1954, employee approval is not yet generally sought in this formal way.

Assignment of Responsibility for Designing the Rating Scale

When a particular type of rating plan has been selected—the classification method, for example—the actual scale must still be designed to fit the jobs which are to be rated. Rarely, if ever, is it possible to take a plan and use it with no adjustments whatsoever. The range of jobs to be rated, the type of jobs included in the

Figure 5.4

RESPONSIBILITY FOR TRAINING
JOB DESCRIPTION INTERVIEWERS

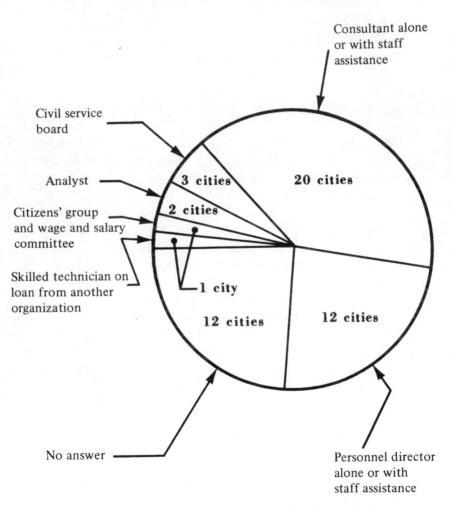

Consultant alone
or with staff
assistance

Civil service
board

Analyst

Citizens' group
and wage and salary
committee

Skilled technician on
loan from another
organization

3 cities

2 cities

1 city

20 cities

12 cities

12 cities

No answer

Personnel director
alone or with
staff assistance

Table 5.5

RESPONSIBILITY FOR WRITING FINAL JOB
DESCRIPTIONS

Title	Number of cities
Consultants	10
Personnel staff	7
Personnel director	5
Classification analyst	5
Civil service department	3
Consultant and personnel director	2
Consultant and staff	2
Consultant and civil service department	1
Assistant personnel director	1
Director and personnel	1
No answer	14
Total	51

range, and any conditions peculiar to the organization in question all affect the rating scale. The best solution is to tailor a plan to fit specific requirements although it is usually constructed according to the basic specifications of the general method chosen.

Those responsible for installing job evaluation programs in municipalities have recognized the need for this step since all respondents replying to the question indicated that they had designed rating plans to fit their particular needs.

Consultants or personnel directors were primarily responsible for designing the rating scale. They were named either alone or with others in all but 5 of the 30 cities answering the question. (See Figure 5.5.) Sixteen instances of consultant responsibility, however, leads the 9 with personnel responsibility.

43

Figure 5.5

RESPONSIBILITY FOR DESIGNING SCALE
USED FOR RATING JOBS

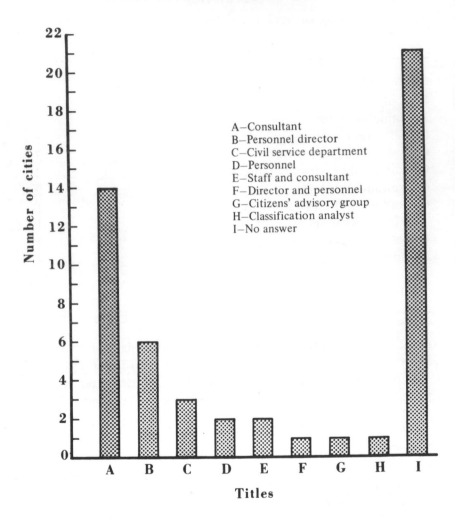

A—Consultant
B—Personnel director
C—Civil service department
D—Personnel
E—Staff and consultant
F—Director and personnel
G—Citizens' advisory group
H—Classification analyst
I—No answer

In the 1954 survey, consultants and personnel directors were used with almost equal frequency. The trend in 1970 was toward the greater use of consultants.

Assignment of Responsibility for Rating Jobs

When the jobs have been described and the rating plan designed, the jobs are ready to be rated. Each job description must be studied carefully by the rater before he can begin the rating process.

In some cases, each rater is asked to rate the jobs independently as the first step in the process. Then the evaluations of each rater are collected, and the raters meet for the purpose of resolving any differences of opinion about the jobs. In other cases, the raters, called together in a group, determine the proper evaluation of each job or the series of jobs under discussion.

Experts in rating techniques generally agree that the best method is to have each rater exercise independent judgment before he meets with the other raters. This plan assures each rater an opportunity to consider each job carefully. Thus, he is not swayed by a more dominating personality in making his first decision. A better evaluation probably will result than where the group rating plan alone is followed.

Sometimes an organization may assign the rating function to one individual. He then evaluates all the jobs under consideration. In such instances, however, his final evaluation is often subject to review by other individuals within the organization.

Here again authorities in the field believe that having several individuals rate the job is a better plan because it tends to eliminate some of the bias that may exist in a single individual. It also provides for greater participation of employees. In turn, this usually leads to a broader understanding of job evaluation, to greater confidence in the work that has been done, and to greater acceptance of the final results.

An analysis of the information in Table 5.6 reveals the variety of practice which occurred with respect to the assignment of

45

Table 5.6

RESPONSIBILITY FOR RATING JOBS

Title	Number of cities
Consultants	12
Personnel director	7
Personnel staff	4
Civil service department	2
Classification analyst	2
Consultant and staff	2
Joint committee	1
Management committee	1
Advisory committee	1
Director and personnel	1
No answer	18
Total	51

responsibility for rating jobs. Twenty-one respondents listed one title, with consultants and personnel directors most frequently cited. Consultants were named in 12 instances and personnel directors in seven. A classification analyst was assigned the role in two cities. Twelve respondents indicated a group or committee performed the rating, although no trend of composition of the membership of the group or committee was reported. If title alone is considered, it would seem that individual rating is more popular than committee rating. However, in actual practice, the respondents may have listed only the lead person and not added those assisting him. Whether or not the raters performed the evaluation independently and then met with other raters to resolve differences of opinion was not specified by any of those organizations indicating more than one rater.

The committee plan of job rating was the most popular approach in 1954. At that time civil service boards, departments, and the like took the lead role. This is in contrast to the 1970 approach of assigning the responsibility more frequently to consultants or personnel directors or to these persons aided by their staffs.

Table 5.7

TYPE OF TRAINING GIVEN JOB RATERS

Type	Number of cities
Studied job evaluation literature	30
Learned procedures for rating	29
Studied rating system chosen	28
Rated sample job descriptions which were criticized	17
Trained by consultants	8
Orientation and on-the-job training	1
Had prior training and experience	2
Total	115*

* Some cities indicated more than one type of training.

Methods Used and Assignment of Responsibility for Training Job Raters

Several methods of training job raters were reported. In many cities more than one method was utilized to provide for a more comprehensive type of training program. The procedures followed and the frequency of their use are shown in Table 5.7. The four most popular approaches, reported by one-third or more of the participants, were (a) studied job evaluation literature, (b) learned

47

Figure 5.6

RESPONSIBILITY FOR TRAINING RATERS

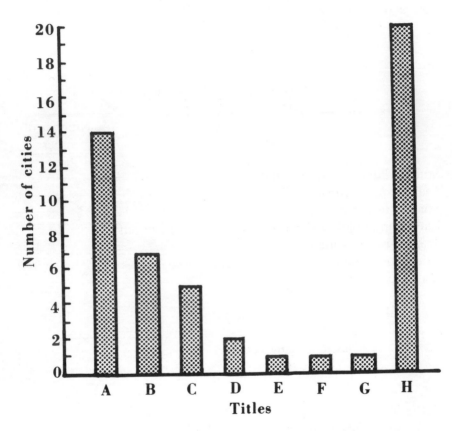

A—Consultant
B—Personnel department
C—Personnel director
D—Civil service department

E—Staff and consultant
F—Director and personnel
G—No training
H—No answer

procedures for rating, (c) studied rating system chosen, and (d) rated sample job descriptions which were criticized.

These same primary methods were used in 1954. Consultants, personnel directors, and members of the personnel department were named most frequently as having been responsible for training job raters. (See Figure 5.6.) Personnel staff members were found to have been more active in this area in the 1970 survey than in 1954. Consultants were prominent in both surveys.

Equalization of Job Ratings

Although every attempt may be made to provide for uniform interpretation and consistency in rating, it cannot be overemphasized that both vertical and horizontal equity must be provided for in the rating plan. Vertical equity means that jobs are ranked in their proper order from low to high for each department and for the organization as a whole. Horizontal equity means that jobs of like responsibility throughout the entire organization are placed at the same level regardless of departmental lines. To assure that such equity does exist, it is usually necessary to cross-check or verify ratings.

The same group which rated the jobs originally may serve also as an equalization committee. In some organizations, such a committee is chosen from higher echelons of management than is the committee that did the original evaluation. This latter plan provides for a review of the work of the first rating group, and it may result in an even higher degree of accuracy than occurs where the same group cross-checks and verifies its own work.

In the majority of the municipalities, the same individual or group responsible for rating the jobs originally also verified the ratings. (See Table 5.8.) The same practice was indicated by those who participated in the 1954 survey.

49

Table 5.8

RESPONSIBILITY FOR EQUALIZING JOBS

Title	Number of cities
Consultants	11
Personnel director	4
Personnel staff	4
Civil service department	3
Classification analyst	3
Consultants and personnel	2
Consultants and staff	2
Director and personnel	1
Joint committee	1
Management committee	1
Advisory committee	1
No answer	18
Total	51

Length of Time Required for Installation

A question often asked by those contemplating a job evaluation installation is, "How long does it take?" Obviously, many factors enter into the length of time required; however, the experience of the municipalities may partially answer the question.

One to two years installation time was reported more frequently than any other span. (See Figure 5.7.) One-half year to a year was next, followed by two to three years, then one-half year or less. Examined in another way, 24 cities of the 37 answering the question (approximately two-thirds) required over one year to install their plans as compared with 13 taking less than one year.

Figure 5.7

LENGTH OF TIME REQUIRED
TO ESTABLISH A JOB
EVALUATION PROGRAM

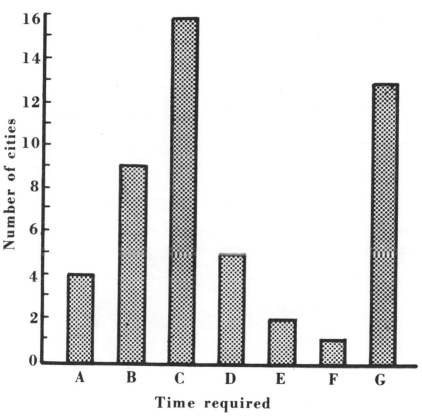

A—0.5 year or less
B—0.6 year to 1 year
C—1 year to 2 years
D—2 years to 3 years

E—3 years to 4 years
F—4 years and over
G—No answer

In 1954, more of the municipalities were found to have completed their plans in six months or less than required over one year. At that time, 15 of the 28 cities reported less than a year, 11 reported over one year, and 2 did not give the length of time. More time for installation, therefore, has become the trend since 1954.

VI

MEASURES TAKEN TO INSURE ACCEPTANCE AND ADVANTAGES GAINED FROM THE PROGRAM

Securing Approval of Top Management

Senior executive officers usually authorize the development of a job evaluation program, and the resulting plan is ordinarily subject to their final approval because any program with such far-reaching effect upon both operation and cost should have top-level approval. Before this group can accept the proposal, it must be informed fully of the results to expect from installation. It is essential that executives be assured that each step in the preparation has been carefully and completely developed. They must know that the jobs have been correctly evaluated, that the rate structure is equitable, and that operation of the plan will not involve costs greater than they are willing to undertake.

Several procedures have been followed by those responsible for presenting their programs to top management. (See Table 6.1.) The most popular method was to hold meetings at which time the

Table 6.1

METHODS USED TO SECURE ACCEPTANCE OF THE JOB EVALUATION PROGRAM

Method	Management occurrence	Supervisor occurrence	Employee occurrence
Meetings	38	36	26
Participation	27	28	21
Individual interviews	24	8	33
Descriptive literature	18	18	17
Memorandum or letter from top city official	18	17	15
Employee publications	5	5	7
Bulletins, letters, memos	–	1	1
Newspaper publicity	–	–	1
Letter from personnel department	1	–	–
Labor negotiations	1	1	1
Civil service rules	1	1	1
Total	133*	115*	123*

* Some cities indicated several methods to secure acceptance of their plan.

details of the program were thoroughly discussed. Thirty-eight of the 51 respondents reported such meetings. Executives participated in the installations in 27 cities, and individual interviews with executives were conducted in 24. In a number of instances, these interviews were supplementary to group meetings. Descriptive literature about the plan, memoranda or letters from the top city official, and stories in employee publications were additional procedures utilized.

The above procedures were the primary ones followed also in 1954, although a slight variation in rank order has occurred since that time. For example, participation was third in popularity in 1954 and second in 1970. Individual interviews were second in popularity in 1954 and third in 1970. No significant trend as far as numbers occurred.

Securing Acceptance of the Supervisory Group

If a program of job evaluation is to function successfully, the supervisory staff must understand and have confidence in it, for they are the individuals who ordinarily recommend increases for employees within its framework. It is very important for supervisors to be thoroughly acquainted with all the details of operation. This need was recognized, and various methods were reported for meeting it. Utilization of more than one technique also was common practice. (See Table 6.1.)

Meetings with supervisors (36 cities), participation in installation (28 cities), descriptive literature about the plan (18 cities), and individual interviews (8 cities) were the major procedures used to inform supervisors.

In 1954, the rank order of procedures was as follows: (a) meetings, (b) individual interviews, (c) participation, (d) descriptive literature, and (e) memoranda or letters from the top city official. The only significant change was in the rank order of "individual interviews." It was in second rank in 1954 with almost two-thirds of the respondents reporting its use. It dropped to fifth rank and approximately one-sixth usage by 1970.

Presentation of Proposed Plan to Employees

Top management and supervisors may be in agreement about the worth of such an installation, but if nonsupervisory workers do not have confidence in its soundness and fairness, an excessive number of grievances and complaints usually will appear. Not only

55

should rank-and-file employees have the program discussed with them at the time the original study is proposed, they also should have the completed plan explained to them in order to win better acceptance and understanding.

Individual interviews, meetings, participation, descriptive literature, and memoranda or letters from the top city official were the five primary procedures used to inform employees. The number of cities using each were 33, 26, 21, 17, and 15, respectively. (See Table 6.1.)

The only change from the above in 1954 was a slight variation in rank order of their popularity. For example, "individual interviews" moved to first rank in 1970 from its second rank in 1954, which caused "meetings" to drop to second rank in 1970.

Methods used to gain approval of executives, supervisors, and employees were basically the same, although some minor variations in frequency of use occurred among the three groups. The personal approach was heavily emphasized with all groups.

General Experience with the Job Evaluation Program

The respondents were asked to indicate their opinions of the plans. (See Figure 6.1.) It is evident from these data that executives who answered this question for the cities believe their plans have been generally satisfactory. If "highly satisfactory" answers are added to the "satisfactory" ones, 44 of the 51 cities have effective programs. In only one case was a "definitely unsatisfactory" plan reported and only 4 cases of "fairly satisfactory."

The respondents in the 1954 survey also reported general satisfaction. Twenty-one of the 28 cities indicated satisfactory or highly satisfactory plans; six indicated fairly satisfactory; and one did not answer the question.

56

Figure 6.1
RELATIVE SATISFACTION WITH JOB EVALUATION PROGRAMS

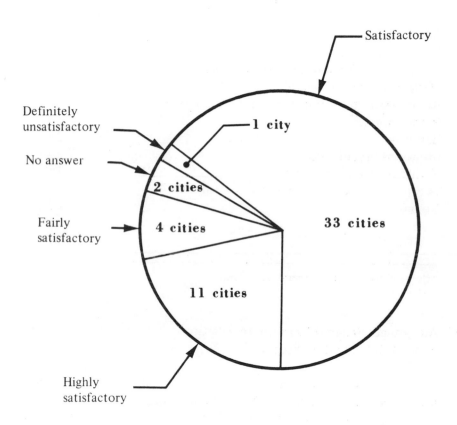

Table 6.2

ADVANTAGES SECURED FROM INSTALLATION
OF JOB EVALUATION

Advantages	Number of cities
Salary equity	46
Consistency, uniformity	43
Factual basis for determining job worth	42
Standardization of salaries	41
Better promotion, transfer, and placement policies	36
Better morale	30
Better control over salary costs	29
Improved organization	29
Reduced employee turnover	18
Greater confidence in civil service commission	1
No answer	2
Total	317*

* Some cities indicated several advantages.

**Advantages Secured from the Installation
of the Job Evaluation Program**

Ten different advantages of having installed job evaluation programs were named, with practically all of the respondents indicating more than one. (See Table 6.2.) An examination of these data reveals that the advantages are similar to those commonly found in other surveys and to those usually cited in the literature on job evaluation.

These same major advantages were reported also by the respondents participating in the 1954 survey.

VII

MAINTAINING AND CONTROLLING THE JOB EVALUATION PROGRAM

Need for Maintenance and Control

Although every effort may be exerted to install a complete, accurate, and usable job evaluation plan, it must be maintained and controlled if it is to continue to serve its purpose effectively.

A static condition seldom exists in any area of activity. It certainly does not occur in the field of job evaluation. For example, the duties and responsibilities of jobs change, and new jobs are created. Requests for reevaluation of jobs already rated may be received either from supervisors or from employees. Job descriptions currently in use must be checked periodically to see that job content actually agrees with the description. Rates and policies of administration require review and adjustment. Factors such as the foregoing necessitate the establishment of procedures and controls for maintaining the program.

59

Table 7.1

**METHODS USED TO MAINTAIN AND CONTROL
JOB EVALUATION PROGRAM**

Method	Number of cities
Supervisors report new jobs to job evaluation division	40
Supervisors report job changes to job evaluation division	38
Periodic wage surveys	36
Periodic reevaluation of all jobs	34
Permanent job evaluation organization for rating jobs	28
Records corrected immediately to record changes	24
Positions evaluated at request of employees, department, director, personnel director, or the city manager	4
Review duties reported on "requisitions for new employee" form	1
Collective bargaining	1
Specifications reviewed for a particular class when requested by department head or before recruitment to fill a vacancy	1
Through a management consulting firm	1
Annual wage index increase based on city area labor market	1
Processing of complaints of employees—unionized and nonunionized	1
Total	210*

* Some cities indicated more than one method.

This need has been recognized in the municipalities. Practically all of the respondents reported that one or more methods have been established to maintain and control their programs.

Methods Used to Maintain and Control Programs

The six procedures used consistently were (a) supervisors report new jobs to the job evaluation division; (b) supervisors report job changes to the job evaluation division; (c) periodic wage surveys are conducted; (d) periodic reevaluations of all jobs are made; (e) permanent job evaluation organization for rating jobs is maintained; and (f) records are corrected immediately to show any change. (See Table 7.1.)

These same six maintenance and control procedures were also the primary ones reported in the 1954 survey.

Assignment of Responsibility for Maintenance and Control

Centralized maintenance and control of the job evaluation plan is exercised in 50 of 51 municipalities in order to help insure that actual operating practices conform as nearly as possible with established procedures.

The personnel department has been assigned the responsibility in over two-thirds of the installations. The civil service board is the next most common assignment since it functions in 8 cities and is combined with the personnel department in one other. The remaining assignments were reported three or less times each. (See Figure 7.1.)

The personnel department and the civil service board, individually or jointly, also exercised overall maintenance and control of the plans studied in 1954. Personnel departments were named by more cities than named civil service boards or commissions at that time also.

61

Figure 7.1

RESPONSIBILITY FOR MAINTENANCE AND CONTROL OF JOB EVALUATION PROGRAM

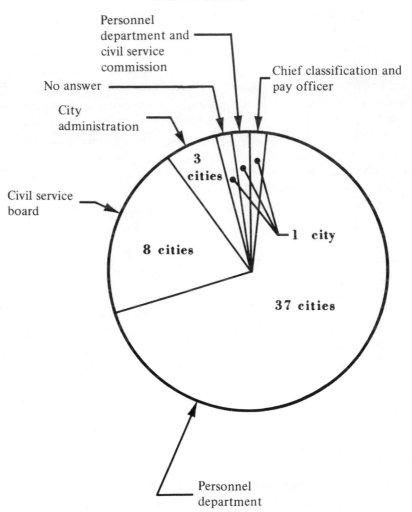

Types of Maintenance and Control Exercised

Several different areas of maintenance and control have been assigned to the central control agency. (See Table 7.2.) The six major ones are:

1. Routing all recommendations for salary increases through the centralized unit in order to check for conformance with plan.
2. Conducting periodic wage surveys.
3. Recommending improvements in the plan.
4. Conducting research to keep abreast of trends in job evaluation.
5. Observing day-to-day functioning in order to determine weaknesses in the plan.
6. Keeping interest alive in the program.

The same areas were primary maintenance and control points at the time of the 1954 survey. However, "keeping alive interest in the program" was in fifth rank at that time while it was in sixth rank in 1970.

Internal Operating Problems Encountered

Although a job evaluation program may be well installed, properly maintained, effectively controlled, and successfully administered, certain problems or difficulties usually arise from time to time to plague those responsible for it. Its dynamic nature is such, however, that problems can be expected. Any plan that affects many persons so vitally is usually subject to a number of difficulties in actual operation.

If the types of problems that do arise are understood and anticipated, and if plans are made in advance to meet them, their undersirable effects often can be minimized.

Three respondents did not answer the question concerning problems encountered. All of the others reported that one or more

63

Table 7.2

TYPES OF MAINTENANCE AND CONTROL EXERCISED BY
CENTRAL CONTROL AGENCY

Type of maintenance and control	Number of cities
All recommended salary increases cleared through centralized unit to check for conformance with plan	43
Conduct periodic wage surveys	40
Recommend improvements in program	32
Research to keep abreast with trends in job evaluation	27
Close observation of day-to-day functioning in order to ascertain weaknesses in plan	23
Keep alive interest in program	15
Systematic review of all classes	1
Collective bargaining	1
Trained to work with consultants	1
Conduct studies of jobs as requested by departments	1
Special survey and periodic spot checking in the field	1
All classification and grade change requests reviewed by personnel department	1
Conduct job classification studies	1
New classes and position reclassifications require review by personnel department and approval of civil service commission	1
Personnel director and staff and bargaining unit representatives continuously examine classifications	1
Total	189*

* Some cities indicated more than one type of control.

problems were encountered. (See Table 7.3.) Those named by at least one-third or more were:

1. Getting changes in jobs and new jobs reported promptly.
2. Insuring uniform interpretation of the program.
3. Receiving pressure to increase individual rates above the maximum rate of the job.
4. Maintaining experienced personnel to administer the plan.

Table 7.3

INTERNAL OPERATING PROBLEMS ENCOUNTERED IN JOB EVALUATION PROGRAMS

Problems encountered	Number of cities
Getting changes in jobs and new jobs reported promptly	37
Insuring uniform interpretation of the program	29
Receiving pressure to increase individual rates above the maximum rate of the job	29
Maintaining experienced personnel to administer the plan	19
Keeping the executive and supervisory group "sold" on job evaluation	14
Keeping everyone informed about changes that occur in the program	14
Handling grievances over rates effectively	9
Maintaining executive participation	8
Guarding against attempts to gain increases for employees through classification changes	1
No answer	3
Total	163*

* Some cities indicated more than one problem.

Four other fairly prevalent problems were (a) keeping the executive and supervisory group "sold" on job evaluation, (b) keeping everyone informed about changes that occur in the program, (c) handling grievances over rates effectively, and (d) maintaining executive participation.

The four problems experienced in at least one-third of the cities were also problems in 1954. However, their rank order differs slightly from the 1970 findings. For example, "receiving pressure to increase individual rates above the maximum" was the most commonly cited problem in 1954 but had dropped down one rank in 1970. "Getting changes in jobs and new jobs reported promptly" ranked as the first problem in 1970 but as the second major one in 1954. Despite the above, no really significant changes occurred.

Utilization of Electronic Data Processing
for Wage and Salary Records and Reports

One of the outstanding developments in the last decade has been the utilization of electronic data processing in many areas of management. Wage and salary administration, with all its myriad records and reports, has been one of the programs which has benefited greatly from this modern management technique.

Municipalities have been among the many organizations throughout the country which have turned to electronic data processing of many types of wage and salary records and reports. EDP is used now in 39 of the 51 cities, will be used in 5 more cities by the end of 1971, and will be added in 5 other cities in the near future. (See Figure 7.2.) One city was the exception; it had no plan to move into EDP.

Many types of records and reports are currently being processed electronically. (See Table 7.4.) Twelve were listed by at least one-half of the participants, two others by at least one-third, and two more by slightly less than one-third. Although the remaining reports were processed in six or less of the

66

Figure 7.2

STATUS OF EDP WAGE AND SALARY ADMINISTRATION RECORDS AND REPORTS

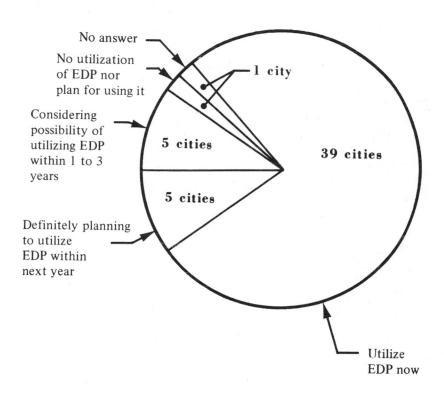

No answer

No utilization of EDP nor plan for using it

1 city

Considering possibility of utilizing EDP within 1 to 3 years

5 cities

5 cities

39 cities

Definitely planning to utilize EDP within next year

Utilize EDP now

municipalities, their titles indicate further possibilities for adaptation to EDP.

No information was secured in the 1954 survey about the utilization of EDP in wage and salary administration.

Table 7.4

WAGE AND SALARY RECORDS AND REPORTS
PROCESSED ELECTRONICALLY

Records and reports	Number of cities
Salary payroll	45
Payroll tax reports such as OASI, income, etc.	43
Deductions from employees' gross earnings	43
Cumulative payroll cost for week, month, year, etc.	42
Payroll registers	41
Pension recipient records showing names, amounts paid, etc.	39
Payroll costs by occupation, department, total organization, etc.	37
Individual employee payroll records	36
Day or hourly payroll	35
Overtime earnings by employee, job, department, etc.	30
Distribution of labor costs by job, department, etc.	26
Fringe benefit cost by type of benefits and totals	26
Average wages or salaries by job grade, job title, etc.	24
Sick leave costs	18
Wage survey data analysis	16
Illness and accident costs	14
Commission earnings of employee, job, department, etc.	6
Job evaluation rating analysis	6
Incentive earning reports	3
Profit sharing and other bonus reports	2

Table 7.4 (continued)

WAGE AND SALARY RECORDS AND REPORTS
PROCESSED ELECTRONICALLY

Records and reports	Number of cities
Budget projections	1
Statistical data for labor negotiations	1
Employee occupation code and department, salary, date of hire, salary range number, and date of last appointment	1
Merit increase advancement eligibility dates	1
Longevity pay eligibility rosters	1
Vacation pay eligibility rosters	1
Sick leave eligibility rosters	1
Seniority dates	1
Length of accumulated service	1
Unit manning document—total "on board," vacancies listing	1
Performance ratings at end of probation	1
Performance rating analysis by factor and division, operational	1
Civil service exam scoring and test history file, operational	1
No answer	4
Total	549*

* Some cities reported processing more than one record and report.

VIII

SUMMARY AND CONCLUSIONS

Summary

In 1954 a survey was made of job evaluation procedures and practices in the field of municipal government. The decision was made in 1970 to reexamine these areas for the purpose of determining what had occurred in the intervening years. The 1970 findings are summarized below together with comparisons, where appropriate, between the two periods.

1. Fifty-one formal job evaluation programs were in effect in the 68 municipalities answering the questionnaires in 1970. Twenty-eight formal plans were found in the 57 cities in the 1954 survey. The increase between the two periods in number of installations is approximately 82 percent.

2. Job evaluation has long been a practice in municipal government administration. Although 2 plans were in effect prior to 1930, the real beginning occurred in the 1930's when 7 plans were installed. The movement gained impetus in the 1940's with

10 more installations. The 1950's and 1960's were also decades of further growth. Fifteen plans were completed in the 1950's and 16 in the 1960's. One plan was completed as recently as in 1970.

3. Various reasons were given for job evaluation installations. The programs were developed most frequently in order (a) to create equity in salary administration, (b) to provide definite, systematic, and factual data for determining the relative worth of jobs, (c) to improve salary administration, (d) to standardize salary administration, and (e) to establish a basis for promotion. These same major reasons for installation were reported in 1954. Their rank order varies slightly from that in 1970, but no significant difference occurred in their relative importance.

4. The original idea for investingating the advantages of a job evaluation program has come primarily from representatives of management in both periods.

5. No one person or group in management predominated as the originator of the idea. The personnel manager, either alone or with others, was named more frequently than anyone else. The above situation also occurred in the earlier study.

6. The source of authority for the installations, both in 1970 and 1954, came primarily from the city council or comparable body, city charters or other types of legislation, or civil service boards or commissions.

7. All of the respondents answering the question recognized the necessity for informing supervisors about the objectives sought and the techniques of administration of job evaluation. The four primary methods used to accomplish these purposes were (a) staff meetings, (b) conferences with individual staff members, (c) departmental or group meetings, and (d) letter or memorandum from the city head. These same methods also were the primary ones used in 1954.

8. The problem of acquainting nonsupervisory employees was approached with similar thoroughness in both 1970 and 1954. The six primary methods used in both periods were (a) information from supervisors or department heads, (b) individual conferences, (c) group meetings, (d) letter or memorandum from

the city head, (e) conferences with employee leaders, and (f) special bulletins and staff reports.

9. The personal approach was used more frequently in both periods to inform both supervisors and employees about the plan than was the impersonal one.

10. The general procedures to be followed in installing the plan, the scope of the program, the advantages to be secured from installation, and its expected effects upon supervisors and employees were the four major areas of emphasis in informing the above groups. These same four areas were emphasized also in the plans reviewed in 1954, although a slight variation in rank order was found between the two periods.

11. Employees of the cities played the dominant role in the installation of job evaluation. Either they were charged with the entire responsibility, or they were in charge but had the assistance of consultants. This trend differs from that found in 1954. At that time, management consultants were in the leadership role more often than were city employees.

12. The two primary reasons for choosing employees to install the plans were (a) they knew the organization better than an outsider, and (b) they were well qualified to perform the work.

13. The personnel department exercised overall responsibility for supervising the job evaluation installation in a large majority of the cities. This same arrangement occurred in 1954.

14. Overall direction of the installation was most commonly assigned to the personnel director. In 1954, consultants, civil service boards, and public administration groups were primarily responsible. Here, as in the previously discussed areas, the personnel director and his department or staff were far more active in supervising and directing job evaluation programs in 1970 than they were sixteen years ago.

15. The principal responsibilities handled in overall direction both in 1954 and 1970 were (a) establishing installation procedures, (b) selecting personnel to carry them out, and (c) maintaining and administering the program as it was being developed.

16. The classification (grade) method for evaluating jobs was used in over half of the municipalities. It was combined with elements of either the rank, point, or factor-comparision methods in eight others. Thus, the procedure was employed to some degree in slightly over two-thirds of the cities. The classification method was used also in over half the cities in rating jobs in the 1954 survey. At that time, too, it was used either alone or was combined with one of the other three plans.

17. The primary reason for the selection of the particular rating plan was that it was better suited to city needs. Slightly over two-thirds of the respondents indicated that their choice was based upon this factor. Three other reasons, reported by at least one-third of the respondents were (a) used by other cities, (b) more easily understood by employees, and (c) recommended by consultant. "Better suited to city needs" also was the primary reason for choosing the rating methods in plans reviewed in 1954. The other three reasons were commonly cited also.

18. The personnel director or a consultant, either operating alone or assisted by others, made the actual selection of the job rating plan in more cities than did any other person or group. The former served in 14 cities and the latter in 13 cities. In 1954 the consultant alone, or aided by others, selected the rating plan more often than anyone else. The rise in the number of personnel directors active in this role parallels their greater involvement in overall direction, supervision, and maintenance of job evaluation plans.

19. Rating beginning jobs through the department or division head level, followed by beginning jobs through the top executive level, and, finally, beginning jobs and up to, but not including, department or division heads was the rank order of popularity of the ranges included in the plans. The same rank order prevailed in 1954.

20. Those responsible for overall direction and coordination in both 1970 and 1954 were responsible also for determining the range of jobs to be included.

21. The six most popular procedures for securing job facts

were (a) interviewing employees on the jobs, (b) interviewing supervisors of the jobs, (c) requesting employees to fill in questionnaires about the jobs, (d) requesting employees to fill in a questionnaire and also interviewing employees, (e) requesting supervisors to fill in questionnaires about the jobs, and (f) requesting supervisors to fill in questionnaires and also interviewing supervisors about the jobs. Approximately the same major overall procedures were used to gather job facts in each of the two studies.

22. The personnel director or consultant, either working alone or assisted by others, was primarily responsible for securing job facts. The former assignment was made in one-third of the cities, while the latter occurred in slightly over one-fourth. Both assignments were used also in 1954, but the personnel director and his staff were more active in 1970 than in 1954.

23. Most frequently, job analysts were trained (a) through the use of job evaluation literature, (b) through direct teaching of procedures for getting job facts, (c) through direct teaching of principles of interviewing, (d) through preparation of sample job descriptions which were criticized, and (e) through university courses. Although these methods were used also in 1954, their rank differs slightly from the above. The relative change is so minor, however, that no new trend is evident.

24. Consultants and personnel directors, either alone or with staff assistance, were cited most frequently as being in charge of the training programs. Consultants served in more cities than did personnel directors in both 1970 and 1954. However, the personnel director and his staff were more active in 1970 than in the preceding period.

25. In the majority of the municipalities, both in 1970 and 1954, the same person who secured the job facts also wrote the job descriptions.

26. Final job descriptions were approved only by supervisors in most of the cities. In 1970, as in 1954, employee approval was not yet generally sought in this formal way.

27. Consultants or personnel directors, either alone or assisted

74

by others, were primarily responsible for designing job rating scales. Consultants were named more frequently than personnel directors. Consultants and personnel directors were almost equal in frequency of performance in 1954. The trend has moved toward the greater use of consultants at the present time.

28. A variety of practice occurred with respect to the assignment of responsibility for rating jobs. However, consultants and personnel directors were named with greater frequency than anyone else. Consultants also served in more cities than did personnel directors. Fewer cities indicated that committees were used to rate than indicated one individual. Committee rating was more popular in 1954.

29. The major procedures followed in training raters in both 1970 and 1954 were (1) studied job evaluation literature, (2) learned procedures for rating, (3) studied the rating system, and (4) rated sample job descriptions which were criticized.

30. Consultants, personnel directors, or other members of the personnel department were primarily responsible for training job raters. Consultants and personnel directors were named with almost equal frequency. Personnel staff also were more active in training in 1970 than they had been in 1954.

31. In the majority of the cities, both in 1970 and 1954, the same individual or group who rated the jobs originally also verified the ratings.

32. Approximately two-thirds of the respondents answering the question stated that it took over one year to install the program. One to two years was the time span checked most frequently. A significant change has occurred in the length of time required for installation since 1954. Six months or less was the typical time requirement in the earlier period.

33. Five major procedures were followed in securing the final adoption of the proposed job evaluation programs by top management. These were (a) meetings with members of top management, (b) participation by top management in phases of the installation, (c) individual interviews with members of top management, (d) distribution of descriptive literature about the

plan, and (e) letter or memorandum from the top city official. Although the rank order of these five procedures varied slightly between the two surveys, the same five were also popular in the first survey.

34. The above five methods also were used in both 1970 and 1954 to win the cooperation and support of the supervisory and nonsupervisory groups. Their rank order differs for top management, supervisory, and nonsupervisory employees, but each was used for the above purposes.

35. Forty-four of the respondents rated their job evaluation plans as satisfactory or highly satisfactory. Thirty-three of the 44 checked the former, and 11 checked the latter. Four plans were reported as fairly satisfactory; one was definitely unsatisfactory. The 1954 respondents also reported general satisfaction. Twenty-one of the 28 checked either satisfactory or highly satisfactory, and 6 indicated fairly satisfactory. No unsatisfactory plan was indicated.

36. The major advantages resulting from the adoption of the plans which were named by over one-half of the cities were (a) salary equity; (b) consistency, uniformity; (c) factual basis for determining job worth; (d) standardization of salaries; (e) better promotion, transfer, and placement policies; (f) better morale; (g) better control over salary costs; and (h) improved organization. These same major advantages were checked also by the respondents participating in the 1954 survey.

37. Once the job evaluation program has been installed, efforts are made to keep it up to date. The five, named by over one-half the cities, were (a) supervisors report new jobs to the job evaluation division, (b) supervisors report job changes to the job evaluation division, (c) periodic wage surveys are conducted, (d) periodic reevaluation of all jobs is made, and (e) permanent job evaluation organization for rating jobs is maintained. A sixth method, "records corrected immediately to record changes," was reported by over one-third of the respondents. These same maintenance procedures were popular in 1954.

38. Centralized control of the program is assigned to the

personnel department in approximately three-fourths of the cities. Joint responsibility with the civil service commission occurs in one other installation. The civil service board and city administration exercise such control in a few cities. Personnel departments also were carrying this responsibility in most of the cities in 1954.

39. The major areas of control, each reported by more than one-third of the respondents, were (a) routing all recommendations for salary increases through the centralized unit, (b) conducting periodic wage surveys, (c) recommending improvements in the plan, (d) conducting research to keep abreast of changes, and (e) observing day-to-day functioning in order to ascertain weaknesses. The only other area, reported by almost one-third of the respondents, was "keeping interest alive." These areas were primary control points also in the earlier installations. However, "keeping interest alive" was in fifth rank in 1954 while it is sixth in the 1970 survey.

40. All of the respondents who replied to the question listed one or more problems which had been encountered in job evaluation administration. The four checked by at least one-third or more were (a) getting changes in jobs and new jobs reported promptly, (b) insuring uniform interpretation of the program, (c) receiving pressure to increase individual rates above maximum, and (d) maintaining experienced personnel to administer the plan.

The above problems were common also in the earlier installations. However, their rank order differs slightly from the 1970 findings. For example, "receiving pressure to increase individual rates above maximum" was the most commonly cited problem in 1954, but "getting changes in jobs and new jobs reported promptly" surpassed it in 1970.

41. Data processing of wage and salary records and reports is widely used in the field of municipal government. In 1970 it was in operation in 35 of the 51 cities. Five more have definite plans to adapt to it in 1971, while five others are considering its possible use within one to three years. One respondent stated that no plans for utilization were under consideration now; another did not answer the question. This area of information was not included in the earlier survey.

77

42. Twelve types of records and reports which were being processed electronically by at least one-half of the cities were (a) salary payroll; (b) payroll taxes such as OASI, etc.; (c) deductions from employee earnings; (d) cumulative payroll cost for week, month, year, etc.; (e) payroll registers; (g) payroll costs by occupation, department, etc.; (h) individual employee payroll records; (i) day or hourly payroll; (j) overtime earnings by employee, job, department, etc.; (k) distribution of labor cost by job, department, etc.; and (l) fringe benefits by type of benefits and totals.

Conclusions

Job evaluation programs apparently have served their cities well in that not only have the earlier plans continued to exist but many more have been installed since 1954.

In most instances, basic procedures and practices have endured the test of time since no radical departures were found when a comparison was made between more recent programs and those installed approximately sixteen years ago.

The only change particularly striking was in the administrative area. Personnel directors and their staffs have become much more active in planning, directing, and controlling various phases of job evaluation installation and administration. Reliance upon consultants is not as prevalent today as it was in 1954. Personnel people appear to be coming more into their own in this vital function of personnel administration.

It is not possible to predict whether or not a new and better approach to determining job rates will occur in the future. In the meantime, the 51 respondents to this survey serve as the judges in their field. The verdict of 44 of them (86 percent) is that their plans are satisfactory to highly satisfactory.

Appendix A

NATIONAL SURVEY OF JOB EVALUATION AND DATA PROCESSING OF
PAYROLL RECORDS PRACTICES IN MUNICIPALITIES

This questionnaire is arranged as a simple check list on your policies and practices of job evaluation, and the extent of your utilization of data processing of
payroll records.

The Bureau of Business Research hereby assures all cooperating concerns that no
individual replies will be made available to others and only the summarized results will
be published.

A number of subheadings are included under many of the statements. Please check
all of them which pertain to the practices in your organization.

Please return promptly to the Bureau of Business Research, The University of
Texas, Austin, Texas.

Name of Organization:
Address:

Name of Respondent:_____Title:_____
Total Number of Employees:_____

1. HISTORICAL BACKGROUND

    1.1 Status of Job Evaluation in your organization
        1.11 Formal plan now in effect
        1.12 Installing a formal plan at present time   _____
        1.13 Informal plan now in effect   _____
        1.14 Definitely planning to install a formal plan in the near   _____
             future
        1.15 Considering possibility of installing a formal plan   _____
        1.16 No job evaluation program in effect or plan to install   _____
        1.17 Plan formerly in effect, but discontinued due to:
            1.171 weakness of installation
            1.172 inadequate administrative organization   _____
            1.173 change in executive personnel   _____
            1.174 union opposition   _____
            1.175 administrative inflexibility   _____
            1.176 other:_____   _____

    1.2 Year in which your program was established_____.

    1.3 Length of time required to install your plan _____.

    1.4 Reasons for installing your job evaluation program:
        1.41 To create equity in salary administration
        1.42 To improve salary administration   _____
        1.43 To standardize salary administration   _____
        1.44 To provide definite, systematic, and factual data for   _____
             determining the relative worth of jobs
        1.45 To control salary costs   _____
        1.46 To establish a basis for placement and promotion   _____
        1.47 To increase employee morale   _____
        1.48 To reduce grievances and turnover   _____
        1.49 Other:_____   _____

1.5 Source of original suggestion for installing your job evaluation program:
    1.51 Personnel manager_____   1.54 Supervisory employees _____
    1.52 Salary committee _____   1.55 Non-supervisory employees _____
    1.53 President   _____   1.56 Other:_____

1.6 Source from which authorization for your job evaluation program was secured:
    1.61 Board of directors   _____   1.63 Executive committee   _____
    1.62 President   _____   1.64 Other: _____

2. TYPE OF JOB EVALUATION PLAN IN USE

2.1 Method chosen by your organization to rate jobs:
    2.11 Rank   _____   2.14 Factor comparison   _____
    2.12 Grade or classification _____   2.15 Other:_____
    2.13 Point   _____

2.2 Reasons for choosing your particular plan of job evaluation:
    2.21 Better suited to company needs   _____
    2.22 Recommended by management consultant   _____
    2.23 Used by other companies in the field   _____
    2.24 Fewer problems of administration   _____
    2.25 More information about the plan   _____
    2.26 More easily understood by all employees   _____
    2.27 Other:_____

3. COMMUNICATION OF INFORMATION ABOUT PLAN

3.1 Methods used to inform supervisors and employees about the proposed job
    evaluation studies:

3.11 Supervisors
    3.111 Staff meetings   _____
    3.112 Departmental group
        meetings_____
    3.113 Conferences with indi-
        vidual staff members _____
    3.114 Letter or memorandum
        from president   _____
    3.115 Other:_____
        _____

3.12 Employees
    3.121 Group meetings   _____
    3.122 Letter or memorandum
        from president   _____
    3.123 Employee publications
    3.124 Conferences with em-
        ployee leaders   _____
    3.125 Union representa-
        tives   _____
    3.126 Information from
        Supervisors   _____
    3.127 Special bulletins   _____
    3.128 Individual conferences
    3.129 Other:_____

3.2 Type of information given to your supervisors and employees about the proposed
    job evaluation studies:
    3.21 Advantages to be secured from the installation   _____
    3.22 General procedures to be followed   _____
    3.23 Scope of the program   _____
    3.24 Effect of program on supervisors and employees   _____
    3.25 Other:_____

4. INSTALLATION OF JOB EVALUATION PROGRAM

4.1 Assignment of responsibility for installation of job evaluation program in your
    organization:
    4.11 Organization employees without aid of management consultant firm   _____
    4.12 Organization employees aided by management consultant firm   _____
    4.13 Management consultant firm exclusively   _____
    4.14 Management consultant firm aided by employees   _____

4.2 Reasons for your choice of the group indicated above:
    4.21 Organization employees (Applies if 4.11 answered above.)
        4.211 Well qualified to install program
        4.212 Knew organization better than an outsider   _____
        4.213 Reduce suspicion toward the plan   _____
        4.214 Participation aid in acceptance and understanding   _____
        4.215 Trains group for maintenance of program   _____
        4.216 Other: _____ _____

    4.22 Management consultant (Applies if 4.13 answered above)
        4.221 Specialist in work_____   4.223 More objective viewpoint ____
        4.222 Save time   _____   4.224 Other: _____

    4.23 Company employees and management consultants working together (Applies
        if 4.12 or 4.14 answered above)
        4.231 Required less time than employees working alone
        4.232 Knowledge of organization combined with technical skill   _____
        4.233 Allows employee participation, but maintains objective
              point of view   _____
        4.234 Other: _____

4.3 Department or area to which those responsible for installing the job evaluation program were assigned:
    4.31 Personnel department   _____   4.34 Organization department   _____
    4.32 President's office   _____   4.35 Planning department   _____
    4.33 Secretary's office   _____   4.36 Other: _____

4.4 Duties and responsibilities of those participating in the study:

Duties Performed	Title of Participant or Group
Responsibility for:	
4.41 overall direction of program	
4.42 establishing procedures for installation, maintenance, and administration	
4.43 selecting personnel to carry out all phases of program	
4.44 securing information for job descriptions	
4.45 training those getting information for job descriptions	
4.46 preparing final job descriptions	
4.47 training raters	
4.48 choosing rating plan	
4.49 designing the scale used for grading	
4.4(10) rating jobs	
4.4(11) equalizing jobs	
4.4(12) determining range of jobs to be included	
4.4(13) determining number of job classes used	
4.4(14) other:	

4.5 Type of training given your job evaluation personnel.
    4.51 Analyst
        4.511 Studied job evaluation literature
        4.512 Took university courses   _____
        4.513 Learned procedures for getting job facts   _____
        4.514 Prepared sample job descriptions which
              were criticized   _____
        4.515 Learned principles of interviewing   _____
        4.516 Other: _____

4.52 **Job rater**
    4.521 Studied job evaluation literature   _____
    4.522 Studied rating system chosen   _____
    4.523 Learned procedures for rating   _____
    4.524 Rated sample job descriptions which
          were criticized   _____
    4.525 Other: _____

4.6 Methods used to secure acceptance of your job evaluation program

	Management	Supervisors	Employees
4.61 Meetings	_____	_____	_____
4.62 Participation	_____	_____	_____
4.63 Descriptive literature	_____	_____	_____
4.64 Memorandum or letter from president	_____	_____	_____
4.65 Individual interviews	_____	_____	_____
4.66 Employee publications	_____	_____	_____
4.67 Other:	_____		

4.7 Range of jobs rated in your program:
    4.71 Covers employees up to, but not including department or division heads.
        (We mean the head of a major activity such as accounting.)   _____
    4.72 Covers employees through department or division heads   _____
    4.73 Covers employees through the top executive level   _____

4.8 Number of employees covered in your job evaluation plan _____

4.9 Number of different job descriptions required (One job description may cover as many as 20 or more people.) _____

4.(10) Factors used to evaluate jobs if your system is the point or factor comparison: (List)

4.(11) Methods used to secure information for your job descriptions:
    4.(11)1 Interviewing employee on job   _____
    4.(11)2 Interviewing supervisor on job   _____
    4.(11)3 Questionnaire filled in by employee   _____
    4.(11)4 Questionnaire filled in by supervisor   _____
    4.(11)5 Questionnaire and interview from employee   _____
    4.(11)6 Questionnaire and interview from supervisor   _____
    4.(11)7 Job description written by department head   _____
    4.(11)8 Job description written by employee   _____
    4.(11)9 Other: _____

4.(12) Final job description approved by: 4(12)1 Supervisor   _____
                                      4(12)2 Employee   _____

4.(13) Number of job classes or grades used in your plan: _____

5. MAINTENANCE OF JOB EVALUATION PROGRAM

5.1 Methods used to insure that your job evaluation program is kept up to date:
    5.11 Supervisors report job changes to job evaluation division
    5.12 Supervisors report new jobs to job evaluation division
    5.13 Permanent job evaluation organization for rating jobs
    5.14 Record corrected immediately to record changes
    5.15 Periodic wage surveys
    5.16 Periodic re-evaluation of all jobs
    5.17 Other:_____

5.2 Manner in which control of job evaluation plan is exercised:
    5.21 Person or area administering centralized control_____.
    5.22 Types of control:
        5.221 All salary increases recommended cleared through centralized unit to check with conformance with plan.
        5.222 Close observation of day-to-day functioning in order to ascertain weaknesses in plan
        5.223 Recommend improvements in program
        5.224 Keep alive interest in program
        5.225 Research to keep abreast with trends in job evaluation
        5.226 Conduct periodic wage surveys
        5.227 Other:_____

5.3 Internal operating problems encountered in your plan:
    5.31 Maintaining experienced personnel to administer plan
    5.32 Maintaining executive participation
    5.33 Keeping the executive and supervisory group "sold" on job evaluation
    5.34 Keeping everyone informed on changes that occur in the program
    5.35 Insuring uniform interpretation of the program
    5.36 Getting changes of jobs and new jobs reported promptly
    5.37 Pressure to increase individual rates above the maximum rate of the job
    5.38 Effective handling of rate grievances

6. GENERAL EXPERIENCE WITH YOUR JOB EVALUATION PROGRAM

6.1 Relative satisfaction and dissatisfaction with your program of job evaluation:
    6.11 Highly satisfactory _____   6.13 Fairly satisfactory _____
    6.12 Satisfactory _____   6.14 Definitely unsatisfactory_____

6.2 Advantages secured from the adoption of job evaluation program:
    6.21 Salary equity
    6.22 Better morale
    6.23 Better promotion, transfer, and placement policies
    6.24 Consistency; uniformity
    6.25 Factual basis for determining the worth of jobs
    6.26 Better control over salary costs
    6.27 Standardization of salaries
    6.28 Reduced employee turnover
    6.29 Improved organization
    6.2(10) Other:_____

7. UTILIZATION OF ELECTRONIC DATA PROCESSING (EDP) FOR WAGE AND SALARY RECORDS
   AND REPORTS

   7.1 Current status of EDP of records and reports
   Utilize EDP now _____
   Definitely planning to
   utilize EDP within next year _____
   Considering possibility of
   utilizing EDP within 1 to 3
   years _____
   No utilization of EDP or
   plan for using it _____
   Year of adoption of EDP _____

   7.2 Wage and salary records and reports processed
   Payroll tax reports such as OASI, income, etc._____
   Payroll costs by occupation, department, total company, etc._____
   Fringe benefit cost by type of benefit and totals_____
   Cumulative payroll cost for week, month, year, etc. _____
   Deductions from employee's gross earnings_____
   Pension recipient record showing names, amounts paid, etc._____
   Average wages or salaries by job grade, job title, etc._____
   Overtime earnings by employee, job, department, etc._____
   Commissions earnings by employee, job, department,etc. _____
   Distribution of labor costs by job, department, etc._____
   Profit sharing and other bonus reports_____
   Individual employee payroll record_____
   Illness and accident costs_____
   Incentive earnings reports_____ Sick leave costs_____
   Payroll register_____ Salary payroll _____
   Day or hourly payroll_____ Wage survey data analyses_____
   Job evaluation rating analyses _____
   Other_____

9846 0089